RUMI & SHAMS QUOTES

THAT WILL EXPAND YOUR MIND

This book is adapted from the Rumi and Shams life.

BURHAN UNVER

Mawlana Jalaluddin Rumi

Who was Rumi?

Maulana Jalaluddin Rumi was a 13th century Persian poet, an Islamic dervish and a Sufi mystic. He is regarded as one of the greatest spiritual masters and poetical intellects. Born in 1207 AD, he belonged to a family of learned theologians. He made use of everyday life's circumstances to describe the spiritual world. Rumi's poems have acquired immense popularity, especially among the Persian speakers of Afghanistan, Iran and Tajikistan. Numerous poems written by the great poet have been translated to different languages.

Rumi's father was Bahā ud-Dīn Walad, a scholar, legal adviser and a spiritualist from Balkh, who was additionally referred to by the adherents of Rumi as Sultan al-Ulama or "Sultan of the Scholars".The most imperative impacts upon Rumi, other than his father, were the Persian artists Attar and Sanai. Rumi communicates his appreciation: "Attar was the spirit, Sanai his eyes twain, And in time thereafter, Came we in their train"

He further appreciates the two in another sonnet: "Attar has traversed the seven cities of Love, We are still at the turn of one street".

Rumi's works are written mostly in Persian, but occasionally he also used Turkish, Arabic, and Greek in his verse. His Mathnawī, composed in Konya, is considered one of the greatest poems of the Persian language.

He is regarded as one of the most popular and accomplished poets of all times, and he has been best selling poet in the United States of America. Rumi's work is so relevant to the modern day world that it trends on internet even to this date.

"A craftsman pulled a reed from the tree bed, cut holes in it, and called it a human being. Since then, it's been wailing a tender agony of parting, never mentioning the skill that gave it life as a flute"

~Rumi

The state of humans after parting from God has been pain and agony.

"A wealth you cannot imagine flows through you. Do not consider what strangers say. Be secluded in your secret heart-house, that bowl of silence."

~Rumi

The wealth is love and energy.
God flows and resides within us.
He can make anything possible
therefore it does not matter what
people say. Stay happy.
Silence is the best respone to anyone
or anything, It has its own vibration.
Trust it!

"Be quiet now and wait. It may be that the ocean one, the one we desire so to move into and become, desires us out here on land a little longer, going our sundry roads to the shore.

All is God's plan.
We are still here on   **~Rumi**
earth because it is his will.

"Dear soul, don't set a high value on someone before they deserve it; You either lose them or ruin yourself…!"

~Rumi

"Die! Die! Die in this love! If you die in this love, Your soul will be renewed. Die! Die! Don't fear the death of that which is known If you die to the temporal, You will become timeless."

~Rumi

"Do not seek water, get thirst."

~Rumi

"Everything you possess of skill, and wealth, and handicraft, wasn't it first merely a thought and a quest?"

~Rumi

"For the thirst to possess your love, is worth my blood a hundred times."

~Rumi

"I will soothe you and heal you, I will bring you roses. I too have been covered with thorns."

~Rumi

"I know you're tired but come, this is the way. "For without you, I swear, the town Has become like a prison to me. Distraction and the mountain And the desert, all I desire."

~Rumi

"If I could repeat it, people passing by would be enlightened and go free."

~Rumi

"If there were no way into God, I would not have lain in the grave of this body so long."

~Rumi

"Love calls – everywhere and always. We're sky bound. Are you coming?"

~Rumi

"Like a sculptor, if necessary, carve a friend out of stone. Realize that your inner sight is blind and try to see a treasure in everyone."

~Rumi

"Love isn't the work of the tender and the gentle; Love is the work of wrestlers. The one who becomes a servant of lovers is really a fortunate sovereign. Don't ask anyone about Love; ask Love about Love . Love is a cloud that scatters pearls."

~Rumi

"Lovers find secret places inside this violent world where they make transactions with beauty."

~Rumi

"Wherever you are, and whatever you do, be in love..."

~Rumi

We carry inside us the wonders we seek outside us.

~Rumi

"The moment you accept what troubles you've been given, the door will open."

~Rumi

"Your heart knows the way. Run in that direction."

~Rumi

"These pains you feel are messengers. Listen to them."

~Rumi

"Stop acting so small. You are the universe in ecstatic motion."

~Rumi

"Love is the bridge between you and everything."

~Rumi

"Only from the heart can you touch the sky."

~Rumi

"Keep silent, because the world of silence is a vast fullness."

~Rumi

"The desire to know your own soul will end all other desires."

~Rumi

"When will you begin that long journey into yourself?"

~Rumi

"Let silence take you to the core of life."

~Rumi

"You are not a drop in the ocean. You are the entire ocean, in a drop."

~Rumi

"Whatever lifts the corners of your mouth, trust that."

~Rumi

"My soul is from elsewhere, I'm sure of that, and I intend to end up there."

~Rumi

"Yesterday I was clever, so I wanted to change the world. Today I am wise, so I am changing myself."

~Rumi

"There is a candle in your heart, ready to be kindled. There is a void in your soul, ready to be filled. You feel it, don't you?"

~Rumi

"Be like a tree and let the dead leaves drop."

~Rumi

"I have been a seeker and I still am, but I stopped asking the books and the stars. I started listening to the teaching of my Soul."

~Rumi

"It's your road and yours alone. Others may walk it with you, but no one can walk it for you."

~Rumi

"Let silence be the art you practice."

~Rumi

"In the blackest of your moments, wait with no fear."

~Rumi

"By God, when you see your beauty you will be the idol of yourself."

~Rumi

"Maybe you are searching among the branches, for what only appears in the roots."

~Rumi

"I want to sing like the birds sing, not worrying about who hears or what they think."

~Rumi

"What matters is how quickly you do what your soul directs."

~Rumi

"The whole universe is contained within a single human being – you."

~Rumi

"The spirit is so near that you can't see it! But reach for it… don't be a jar, full of water, whose rim is always dry. Don't be the rider who gallops all night and never sees the horse that is beneath him."

~Rumi

"Take someone who doesn't keep score, who's not looking to be richer, or afraid of losing, who has not the slightest interest even in his own personality: he's free."

~Rumi

"When the world pushes you to your knees, you're in the perfect position to pray."

~Rumi

"Be full of sorrow, that you may become hill of joy; weep, that you may break into laughter."

~Rumi

"There is a voice that doesn't use words, listen."

~Rumi

"In silence there is eloquence. Stop weaving and see how the pattern improves."

~Rumi

"I am not this hair, I am not this skin, I am the soul that lives within."

~Rumi

"Close your eyes, fall in love, stay there. (This is one of my favorite quote. Leave a reply here and let me know what's yours!)"

~Rumi

"What you seek is seeking you."

~Rumi

"Let the beauty we love be what we do."

~Rumi

"There are hundreds of ways to kneel and kiss the ground."

~Rumi

"Run from what's comfortable. Forget safety. Live where you fear to live. Destroy your reputation. Be notorious. I have tried prudent planning long enough. From now on I'll be mad."

~Rumi

"Your task is not to seek for love, but merely to seek and find all the barriers within yourself that you have built against it."

~Rumi

"Sell your cleverness and buy bewilderment. Cleverness is mere opinion. Bewilderment brings intuitive knowledge."

~Rumi

"Very little grows on jagged rock. Be ground. Be crumbled, so wild flowers will come up where you are."

~Rumi

"The lion is most handsome when looking for food."

~Rumi

"If all you can do is crawl, start crawling."

~Rumi

"Let yourself be silently drawn by the stronger pull of what you really love.Raise your words, not voice. It is rain that grows flowers, not thunder."

~Rumi

"When you do things from your soul, you feel a river moving in you, a joy."

~Rumi

"Life is balance of holding on and letting go."

~Rumi

SHORT RUMI QUOTES

Patience is the key to joy.

If light is in your heart, you will find your way home.

Set your life on fire. Seek those who fan your flames.

Dance until you shatter yourself.

Be empty of worrying. Think of who created thought.

As you start to walk on the way, the way appears.

Become the sky. Take an axe to the prison wall. Escape.

Let yourself become living poetry.

Be drunk with love, for love is all that exists.

Be soulful. Be kind. Be in love.

Be an empty page, untouched by words.

I know you're tired but come, this is the way.

The wealth within you, your essence, is your kingdom.

To praise the sun is to praise your own eyes.

What hurts you, blesses you. Darkness is your candle
Respond to every call that excites your spirit.

Wherever you stand, be the soul of that place.

You were born with wings. Why prefer to crawl through life?

Half-heartedness doesn't reach into majesty.

Look at the moon in the sky, not the one in the lake.

What is planted in each person's soul will sprout.

The source of now is here.

Grace comes to forgive and then forgive again.

INSPIRATIONAL RUMI QUOTES

You are not meant for crawling, so don't. You have wings. Learn to use them and fly.

Anyone who genuinely and consistently with both hands looks for something, will find it.

In each moment the fire rages, it will burn away a hundred veils. And carry you a thousand steps toward your goal.

There is a life-force within your soul, seek that life. There is a gem in the mountain of your body, seek that mine. O traveller, if you are in search of that, don't look outside, look inside yourself and seek that.

With every breath, I plant the seeds of devotion, I am a farmer of the heart.

Everyone has been made for some particular work, and the desire for that work has been put in every heart.

Achieve some perfection yourself, so that you may not fall into sorrow by seeing the perfection in others.

Don't be satisfied with stories, how things have gone with others. Unfold your own myth.

Whether one moves slowly or with speed, the one who is a seeker will be a finder.

Be a lamp, or a lifeboat, or a ladder. Help someone's soul heal. Walk out of your house like a shepherd.

Let us carve gems out of our stony hearts and let them light our path to love.

Start a huge, foolish project, like Noah… it makes absolutely no difference what people think of you.

Seek the wisdom that will untie your knot. Seek the path that demands your whole being

Whoever has heart's doors wide open, could see the sun itself in every atom.

The message behind the words is the voice of the heart.

You are not one you are a thousand. Just light your lantern.

DEEP AND EMOTIONAL RUMI QUOTES

If you are irritated by every rub, how will your mirror be polished?

I have neither a soul nor a body, for I come from the very Soul of all souls.

When someone beats a rug, the blows are not against the rug, but against the dust in it.

Concentrate on the Essence, concentrate on the light.

Why do you stay in prison when the door is so wide open?

Beyond the rightness or wrongness of things there is a field, I'll meet you there.

Something opens our wings. Something makes boredom and hurt disappear. Someone fills the cup in front of us: We taste only sacredness.

Every need brings what's needed. Pain bears its cure like a child. Having nothing produces provisions. Ask a difficult question, and the marvelous answer appears.

The soul has been given its own ears to hear things mind does not understand.

Discard yourself and thereby regain yourself. Spread the trap of humility and ensnare love.

All that you think is rain is not. Behind the veil angels sometimes weep.

Inside any deep asking is the answering.

Wisdom tells us we are not worthy; love tells us we are. My life flows between the two.

My words are like a ship, and the sea is their meaning. Come to me and I will take you to the depths of spirit. I will meet you there.

Ignore those that make you fearful and sad, that degrade you back towards disease and death.

The time has come to turn your heart into a temple of fire.

Open your hands if you want to be held.

Be melting snow. Wash yourself of yourself.

The soul is here for its own joy.

WISE RUMI QUOTES (WORDS OF WISDOM)

Conventional opinion is the ruin of our souls.

Whatever purifies you is the right path, I will not try to define it.

Let go of your mind and then be mindful. Close your ears and listen.

The world is a mountain, in which your words are echoed back to you.
Laugh as much as you breathe. Love as long as you live.

All your anxiety is because of your desire for harmony. Seek disharmony,
then you will gain peace.

Anything which is more than our necessity is poison. It may be power, wealth,
hunger, ego, greed, laziness, love, ambition, hate or anything.

Poetry can be dangerous, especially beautiful poetry, because it gives the illusion of having had the experience without actually going through it.

In their seeking, wisdom and madness are one and the same. On the path of love, friend and stranger are one and the same.

Clean out your ears, don't listen for what you already know.

O, happy the soul that saw its own faults.

When you lose all sense of self, the bonds of a thousand chains will vanish.

Peaceful is the one who's not concerned with having more or less. Unbound by name and fame, he is free from sorrow from the world and mostly from himself.

Two there are who are never satisfied – the lover of the world and the lover of knowledge.

Whenever they rebuild an old building, they must first of all destroy the old one.

Your radiance shines in every atom of creation yet our petty desires keep it hidden.

Everything about yesterday has gone with yesterday. Today, it is needed to say new things.

Why are you knocking at every door? Go, knock at the door of your own heart.

RUMI QUOTES ABOUT LOVE, MARRIAGE, PASSION

Lovers don't finally meet somewhere. They're in each other all along.

May these vows and this marriage be blessed.
You have within you more love than you could ever understand.

When you seek love with all your heart you shall find its echo in the universe.

If you want to win hearts, sow the seeds of Love. If you want heaven, stop scattering thorns on the road.

This is love: to fly toward a secret sky, to cause a hundred veils to fall each moment. First to let go of life. Finally, to take a step without feet.

Let yourself be drawn by the stronger pull of that which you truly love.

The minute I heard my first love story I started looking for you, not knowing how blind that was. Lovers don't finally meet somewhere. They're in each other all along.

Goodbyes are only for those who love with their eyes. Because for those who love with heart and soul there is no such thing as separation.

When I am with you, we stay up all night. When you're not here, I can't go to sleep.

There is no salvation for the soul but to fall in love. Only lovers can escape out of these two worlds.

This is what love does and continues to do. It tastes like honey to adults and milk to children.

I once had a thousand desires. But in my one desire to know you all else melted away.

I have no companion but Love, no beginning, no end, no dawn. The soul calls from within me: 'You, ignorant of the way of Love, set me free.'

On the path of love we are neither masters nor the owners of our lives. We are only a brush in the hand of the master painter.

Whatever happens, just keep smiling and lose yourself in love.

This sky where we live is no place to lose your wings so love, love, love.

Why ever talk of miracles when you are destined to become infinite love.

When we practice loving kindness and compassion we are the first ones to profit.

I am yours. Don't give myself back to me.

If you love someone, you are always joined with them – in joy, in absence, in solitude, in strife.

Let your teacher be love itself.

This is a subtle truth. Whatever you love, you are.

There is a path from me to you that I am constantly looking for.

Every moment is made glorious by the light of love.

Now I am sober and there's only the hangover and the memory of love.

RUMI QUOTES ABOUT LIFE, HAPPINESS, WORRYING, JOY

Travel brings power and love back into your life.

Why should I be weary when every cell of my body is bursting with life?

Tend to your vital heart, and all that you worry about will be solved.

Caught by our own thoughts, we worry about everything.

Do not worry if all the candles in the world flicker and die. We have the spark that starts the fire.

Come out of the circle of time and into the circle of love.

This being human is a guest house. Every morning is a new arrival. A joy, a depression, a meanness, some momentary awareness comes as an unexpected visitor... Welcome and entertain them all. Treat each guest honorably. The dark thought, the shame, the malice, meet them at the door laughing, and invite them in. Be grateful for whoever comes, because each has been sent as a guide from beyond.

When I run after what I think I want, my days are a furnace of distress and anxiety; If I sit in my own place of patience, what I need flows to me, and without any pain. From this I understand that what I want also wants me, is looking for me and attracting me. There is a great secret in this for anyone who can grasp it.

There is a life in you, search that life, search the secret jewel in the mountain of your body.

Observe the wonders as they occur around you. Don't claim them. Feel the artistry moving through and be silent.

Don't grieve. Anything you lose comes round in another form.

Oh soul, you worry too much. You have seen your own strength. You have seen your own beauty. You have seen your golden wings. Of anything less, why do you worry? You are in truth the soul, of the soul, of the soul.

My head is bursting with the joy of the unknown. My heart is expanding a thousand fold.

Why should I be unhappy? Every parcel of my being is in full bloom.

Oh! Joy for he who has escaped from this world of perfumes and color! For beyond these colors and these perfumes, these are other colors in the heart and the soul.

Be grateful for your life, every detail of it, and your face will come to shine like a sun, and everyone who sees it will be made glad and peaceful.

The illuminated life can happen now, in the moments left. Die to your ego, and become a true human being.

Travelers, it is late. Life's sun is going to set. During these brief days that you have strength, be quick and spare no effort of your wings.

If destiny comes to help you, love will come to meet you. A life without love isn't a life.

When you feel a peaceful joy, that's when you are near truth. Joy lives concealed in grief.

Don't make yourself miserable with what is to come or not to come.

I learned that every mortal will taste death. But only some will taste life.

With life as short as a half-taken breath, don't plant anything but love.

Be kind and honest, and harmful poisons will turn sweet inside you.

If you want money more than anything, you'll be bought and sold your whole life.

Listen to the unstruck sounds, and what sifts through that music.

QUOTES BY RUMI ON FRIENDSHIP

Your heart and my heart are very, very old friends.

My heart, sit only with those who know and understand you.

There is nothing I want but your presence. In friendship, time dissolves.

Let's rise above this animalistic behavior and be kind to one another.

Be a helpful friend, and you will become a green tree with always new fruit, always deeper journeys into love.

Stay with friends who support you in these. Talk with them about sacred texts, and how you are doing, and how they are doing, and keep your practices together.

Always search for your innermost nature in those you are with, as rose oil imbibes from roses.

My friend, the sufi is the friend of the present moment. To say tomorrow is not our way.

A warm, rainy day-this is how it feels when friends get together. Friend refreshes friend then, as flowers do each others, in a spring rain.

Words are a pretext. It is the inner bond that draws one person to another, not words.

Friendship of the wise is good; a wise enemy is better than a foolish friend.

If you are looking for a friend who is faultless, you will be friendless.

Why struggle to open a door between us when the whole wall is an illusion?

Friend, our closeness is this: anywhere you put your foot, feel me in the firmness under you.

Be with those who help your being.

QUOTES BY RUMI ON SADNESS, HEALING, PAIN, DEATH, LOSS, GRIEF

Whenever sorrow comes, be kind to it. For God has placed a pearl in sorrow's hand.

What hurts you, blesses you. Darkness is your candle.

Your depression is connected to your insolence and refusal to praise.

Don't grieve. Anything you lose comes round in another form.

This place is a dream. Only a sleeper considers it real. Then death comes like dawn, and you wake up laughing at what you thought was your grief.

Don't dismiss the heart, even if it's filled with sorrow. God's treasures are buried in broken hearts.

Don't be sad! Because God sends hope in the most desperate moments. Don't forget, the heaviest rain comes out of the darkest clouds.

Whatever sorrow shakes from your heart, far better things will take their place.

Sorrow prepares you for joy. It violently sweeps everything out of your house, so that new joy can find space to enter. It shakes the yellow leaves from the bough of your heart, so that fresh, green leaves can grow in their place.

Sorrow... It pulls up the rotten roots, so that new roots hidden beneath have room to grow. Whatever sorrow shakes from your heart, far better things will take their place.

Join the community of saints and know the delight of your own soul. Enter the ruins of your heart and learn the meaning of humility.

Grief can be the garden of compassion. If you keep your heart open through everything, your pain can become your greatest ally in your life's search for love and wisdom.

The wound is the place where the light enters you.

Whoever finds love beneath hurt and grief disappears into emptiness with a thousand new disguises.

But listen to me. For one moment quit being sad. Hear blessings dropping their blossoms around you.

Everyone is overridden by thoughts; that's why they have so much heartache and sorrow.

One of the marvels of the world: The sight of a soul sitting in prison with the key in its hand.

Don't turn away. Keep your gaze on the bandaged place. That's where the light enters you.

Don't get lost in your pain, know that one day your pain will become your cure.

Be patient where you sit in the dark. The dawn is coming.

Where there is ruin, there is hope for a treasure.

Suffering is a gift; in its hidden mercy.

Greed makes man blind and foolish, and makes him an easy prey for death.

QUOTES BY RUMI ON PEACE, INNER PEACE, GRATITUDE, SILENCE

Do you pay regular visits to yourself? Start now.

Prayer clears the mist and brings back peace to the soul.

Make peace with the universe. Take joy in it.

Do good to the people for the sake of God or for the peace of your own soul that you may always see what is pure and save your heart from the darkness of hate.

If you could get rid of yourself just once, the secret of secrets would open to you. The face of the unknown, hidden beyond the universe would appear on the mirror of your perception.

Our greatest strength lies in the gentleness and tenderness of our heart.
A little while alone in your room will prove more valuable than anything else
that could ever be given you.

This silence, this moment, every moment, if it's genuinely inside you, brings
what you need. There's nothing to believe. Only when I stopped believing in
myself did I come into this beauty. Sit quietly, and listen for a voice that will
say, 'Be more silent.' Die and be quiet.

Quietness is the surest sign that you've died. Your old life was a frantic
running from silence. Move outside the tangle of fear-thinking. Live in
silence.

A wealth you cannot imagine flows through you. Do not consider what
strangers say. Be secluded in your secret heart-house, that bowl of silence.

Stop, open up, surrender the beloved blind silence. Stay there until you see
you're looking at the light with infinite eyes.

When all your desires are distilled; You will cast just two votes – to love more, and be happy.

Whatever happens to you, don't fall in despair. Even if all the doors are closed, a secret path will be there for you that no one knows. You can't see it yet but so many paradises are at the end of this path…Be grateful! It is easy to thank after obtaining what you want, thank before having what you want.

My dear heart, never think you are better than others. Listen to their sorrows with compassion. If you want peace, don't harbor bad thoughts, do not gossip and don't teach what you do not know.

Everything is emptiness. Everything else, accidental. Emptiness brings peace to your loving. Everything else, disease. In this world of trickery, emptiness is what your soul wants.

There is one way of breathing that is shameful and constricted. Then, there's another way: a breath of love that takes you all the way to infinity.

That which is false troubles the heart, but truth brings joyous tranquility.

Today, let us swim wildly, joyously in gratitude.

Wear gratitude like a cloak and it will feed every corner of your life.

Thankfulness brings you to the place where the beloved lives.

Make peace with the universe. Take joy in it. It will turn to gold. Resurrection will be now. Every moment, a new beauty.

QUOTES BY RUMI ON BEAUTY, UNIVERSE

Do not feel lonely, the entire universe is inside you.

Everything in the universe is within you. Ask all from yourself.

The only lasting beauty is the beauty of the heart.

Shine like the whole universe is yours.

Everything that is made beautiful and fair and lovely is made for the eye of one who sees.

On a day when the wind is perfect, the sail just needs to open and the world is full of beauty. Today is such a day.

The very center of your heart is where life begins. The most beautiful place on earth. The sky will bow down to your beauty, if you do.

You have forgotten the One who doesn't care about ownership, who doesn't try to turn a profit from every human exchange.

The universe and the light of the stars come through me.

The beauty you see in me is a reflection of you.

RUMI QUOTES ON NATURE, OCEAN, WATER, LIGHT, THE SUN, MOON

Your light is more magnificent than sunrise or sunset.

The breeze at dawn has secrets to tell you. Don't go back to sleep.

What hurts the soul? To live without tasting the water of its own essence.

We can't help being thirsty, moving toward the voice of water.

When water gets caught in habitual whirlpools, dig a way out through the bottom of the ocean.

There is a moon inside every human being. Learn to be companions with it.

Who could be so lucky? Who comes to a lake for water and sees the reflection of moon.

Be like the sun for grace and mercy. Be like the night to cover others' faults. Be like running water for generosity. Be like death for rage and anger. Be like the Earth for modesty. Appear as you are. Be as you appear.

Daylight, full of small dancing particles and the one great turning, our souls are dancing with you, without feet, they dance. Can you see them when I whisper in your ear?

You have no need to travel anywhere – journey within yourself. Enter a mine of rubies and bathe in the splendor of your own light.

If you wish to shine like day, burn up the night of self-existence. Dissolve in the Being who is everything.

Your heart is the size of an ocean. Go find yourself in its hidden depths.

Let the waters settle and you will see the moon and the stars mirrored in your own being.

Wherever water flows, life flourishes: wherever tears fall, divine mercy is shown.

How do I know who I am or where I am? How could a single wave locate itself in an ocean.

I have found the heart and will never leave this house of light.

Don't you know yet? It is your Light that lights the worlds.

Don't you know yet? It is your Light that lights the worlds.

Your task? To work with all the passion of your being to acquire an inner light.

Truth lifts the heart, like water refreshes thirst.

Love is the water of life, jump into this water.

Listen to the sound of waves within you.

RUMI QUOTES ON DANCE

We rarely hear the inward music, but we're all dancing to it nevertheless.

Whosoever knoweth the power of the dance, dwelleth in God.

Dancing is when you rise above both worlds, tearing your heart to pieces and giving up your soul.

Without love, all worship is a burden, all dancing is a chore, all music is mere noise.

In your light I learn how to love. In your beauty, how to make poems. You dance inside my chest where no-one sees you, but sometimes I do, and that sight becomes this art.

Dance, when you're broken open. Dance, if you've torn the bandage off. Dance in the middle of the fighting. Dance in your blood. Dance when you're perfectly free.

A divine dance appears in the soul and the body at the time of peace and union. Anyone can learn the dance, just listen to the music.

Dancing is not just getting up painlessly, like a leaf blown on the wind; dancing is when you tear your heart out and rise out of your body to hang suspended between the worlds.

Be kind to yourself, dear – to our innocent follies. Forget any sounds or touch you knew that did not help you dance. You will come to see that all evolves us.

In order to understand the dance one must be still. And in order to truly understand stillness one must dance.

Dance where you can break yourself up to pieces and totally abandon your worldly passions.

Dance, and make joyous the love around you. Dance, and your veils which hide the Light shall swirl in a heap at your feet.

We came whirling out of nothingness, scattering stars like dust... The stars made a circle, and in the middle, we dance.

I am a drunkard from another kind of tavern. I dance to a silent tune. I am the symphony of stars.

There are many ways to the Divine. I have chosen the ways of song, dance, and laughter.

RUMI QUOTES ON HOPE, STRENGTH, TRUST, FEAR, CHANGE

There are a thousand ways to kneel and kiss the ground; there are a thousand ways to go home again.

The Prophets accept all agony and trust it. For the water has never feared the fire.

Put your thoughts to sleep, do not let them cast a shadow over the moon of your heart. Let go of thinking.

It is certain that an atom of goodness on the path of faith is never lost.

On what is fear: Non-acceptance of uncertainty. If we accept that uncertainty, it becomes an adventure!

When you go through a hard period, when everything seems to oppose you, when you feel you cannot even bear one more minute, never give up! Because it is the time and place that the course will divert!

Those who don't feel this love pulling them like a river, those who don't drink dawn like a cup of springwater or take in sunset like a supper, those who don't want to change, let them sleep.

Always remember you are braver than you believe, stronger than you seem, smarter than you think and twice as beautiful as you'd ever imagined.

Why are you so enchanted by this world, when a mine of gold lies within you?

You were born with potential. You were born with goodness and trust. You were born with ideals and dreams. You were born with greatness. You were born with wings.

You are not meant for crawling, so don't. You have wings. Learn to use them and fly.

If something makes you happy in this world, you should think of what will happen to you if that thing were taken away.

If reason dominates in man, he rises higher than angels. If lust overpowers man, he descends lower than the beast.

Move, but don't move the way fear makes you move.

The garden of the world has no limits except in your mind

Looking up gives light, although at first it makes you dizzy.

RUMI SAYINGS ON GOD, SPIRITUALITY, RELIGION

I searched for God and found only myself. I searched for myself and found only God.

Silence is the language of God, all else is poor translation.

Each moment contains a hundred messages from God.

Touched. How did you get here? Close your eyes… and surrender!

Would you become a pilgrim on the road of love? The first condition is that you make yourself humble as dust and ashes.

Love is the water of life. Everything other than love for the most beautiful God is agony of the spirit, though it be sugar-eating. What is agony of the spirit? To advance toward death without seizing hold of the water of life.

If in thirst you drink water from a cup, you see God in it. Those who are not in love with God will see only their own faces in it.

To become spiritual, you must die to self, and come alive in the Lord. Only then will the mysteries of God fall from your lips. To die to self through self-discipline causes suffering but brings you everlasting life.

There is a loneliness more precious than life. There is a freedom more precious than the world. Infinitely more precious than life and the world is that moment when one is alone with God.

Knock, and He'll open the door. Vanish, and He'll make you shine like the sun. Fall, and He'll raise you to the heavens. Become nothing, and He'll turn you into everything.

Sit quietly and listen for a voice that will say, "Be more silent." As that happens, your soul starts to revive.

Till man destroys "self" he is no true friend of God.

Now be silent. Let the One who creates the words speak. He made the door. He made the lock. He also made the key.

Ways of worshipping are not to be ranked as better or worse than one another… It's all praise, and it's all right.

We are all the same… all the same… longing to find our way back… back to the One… back to the only One!

Why, when God's world is so big, did you fall asleep in a prison, of all places?

God turns you from one feeling to another and teaches by means of opposites so that you will have two wings to fly, not one

Stay in the spiritual fire. Let it cook you.

All religions. All this singing. One song. Peace be with you.

I am in the House of Mercy, and my heart is a place of prayer.

RUMI POEMS ABOUT LOVE, LIFE

Poem #1

Love came and became like blood in my body.
It rushed through my veins and encircled my heart.

Poem #2

I will be waiting here…
For your silence to break,
for your soul to shake,
for your love to wake.

Poem #3

I was dead, then alive.
Weeping, then laughing.
The power of love came into me,
and I became fierce like a lion,
then tender like the evening star.

Poem #4

I choose to love you in silence, for in silence I find no rejection.
I choose to love you in loneliness, for in loneliness no one owns you but me.
I choose to adore you from a distance. For distance will shield me from pain.
I choose to kiss you in the wind, for the wind is gentler than my lips.
I choose to hold you in my dreams, for me in dreams, you have no ends.

Poem #5

I have lived on the lip of insanity,
wanting to know reasons,
knocking on a door.
It opens.
I've been knocking from the inside.

Poem #6

I've been looking for a long, long time,
for this thing called love,
I've ridden comets across the sky,
and I've looked below and above.
Then one day I looked inside myself,
and this is what I found,
a golden sun residing there,
beaming forth God's light and sound.

Poem #7

I am so close, I may look distant.
So completely mixed with you, I may look separate.
So out in the open, I appear hidden.
So silent, because I am constantly talking with you.

Poem #8

I was a tiny bug.
Now a mountain.
I was left behind.
Now honored at the head.
You healed my wounded hunger and anger,
and made me a poet who sings about joy.

Poem #9

Sometimes in order to help He makes us cry.
Happy the eye that sheds tears for His sake.
Fortunate the heart that burns for His sake.
Laughter always follow tears.
Blessed are those who understand.
Life blossoms wherever water flows.
Where tears are shed divine mercy is shown

Poem #10

Doing as others told me, I was blind.
Coming when others called me, I was lost.
Then I left everyone, myself as well.
Then I found everyone, myself as well.

Poem #11

This is how it always is when I finish a poem.
A great silence overcomes me
and I wonder why I ever thought to use language.

Shams Tabrizi

Who was Shams

Hazrat Shams was born at some point in the 1180s in Tabriz (present-day Iran). Tabriz was popular among Sufis and many great Sufi saints.

From a young age, he was gifted with spiritual abilities which his parents could not comprehend.

His father was said to be a good man of generous nature, although he was not on the spiritual path and thus Hazrat Shams was unable to reveal his mystic visions to him. This resulted Hazrat Shams feeling estranged from his father and others because he could not explain his spiritual sensibilities to those around him.

He says in his Maqalat:

"My father didn't understand me at all. I was a stranger in my own town. My father was a stranger to me and my heart recoiled from him. I thought he might fall upon me. He'd speak kindly to me, but I thought he'd beat me and expel me from the house. (Maqalat 740) "

When his father would tell him that he didn't understand his ways, Hazrat Shams would answer by telling him that they were not "cut of the same cloth".

For about thirty or forty days just before he reached adolescence, his progress on the spiritual path made him averse to food, and he would hide food in his sleeve whenever it was offered to him.

Journey of Shams

After leaving Tabriz, Hazrat Shams traveled through various places including Baghdad, Damascus, Aleppo, Kayseri, Aksaray, Sivas, Erzurum and Erzincan.

He travelled hidden from the people, constantly striving to guard his miracles and mysteries. Rather than boarding in Sufi lodges, which would provide free hospitality, Hazrat Shams acted and dressed like merchants and would thus stay in inns, which he would have to pay for. In every inn that he stayed, he would put a huge lock on his door, although within the room itself there was nothing but a straw mat.

Even though he ate very little and often went without food for several days, he still needed a source of income to cover his expenses during his travels. Therefore, he would teach children how to read the Quran and even developed a method for teaching the whole Quran in a mere three months.

Shams' first encounter with Rumi

On 15 November 1244, a man came to the famous square of Konya. His name was Shams Tabrizi. He was claiming to be a travelling merchant. As it was said in Haji Bektash Veli's book, "Makalat", he was looking for something which he was going to find in Konya. He saw Rumi riding a horse.

In the marketplace of Konya, amid the cotton stalls, sugar vendors, and vegetable stands, Rumi rode through the street, surrounded by his students. Shams caught hold of the reins of his horse and rudely challenged the master with two questions.

Shams asks Rumi:
"Who was the greater mystic, Bayazid (a Sufi saint) or Hz.Muhammad (s.a.v)?" Shams demanded.

Rumi replied:
"What a strange question! Muhammad is greater than all the saints,"

Shams asked:
"So, why is it then that Muhammad said to God, 'I didn't know you as I should have,' while Bayazid proclaimed, 'Glory be to me! How exalted is my Glory!"

Rumi explained:

That Muhammad was the greater of the two, because Bayazid could be filled to capacity by a single experience of divine blessings. He lost himself completely and was filled with God. Muhammad's capacity was unlimited and could never be filled. His desire was endless, and he was always thirsty. With every moment he came closer to God, and then regretted his former distant state.

For that reason he said, "I have never known you as I should have." It is recorded that after this exchange of words, Rumi felt a window open at the top of his head and saw smoke rise to heaven. He cried out, fell to the ground, and lost consciousness for one hour.

Shams, upon hearing these answers, realized that he was face to face with the object of his longing, the one he had prayed God to send him. When Rumi awoke, he took Shams's hand, and the two of them returned to Rumi's dervish lodge together on foot.

After several years with Rumi in Konya, Shams left and settled in Khoy. As the years passed, Rumi attributed more and more of his own poetry to Shams as a sign of love for his departed friend and master. In Rumi's poetry Shams becomes a guide of Allah's love for mankind; Shams was a sun ("Shams" means "Sun" in Arabic) shining the Light of Sun as guide for the right path dispelling darkness in Rumi's heart, mind, and body on earth.

All facts underline the fact that Tabrizi's search for a disciple ended with Rumi. Rumi was an accomplished scholar and a respected teacher himself so the relationship was not of a typical one between a student and teacher; rather, it was a relationship of mutual respect, brotherhood and friendship.

Shams advised Rumi that Sufism could not be learnt through books but by "going and doing". In the company of Shams, the scholarly Maulana Rumi became spiritually transformed.

The two mystics became inseparable and lived together for many months. With Tabrizi becoming the one focus of his life, Rumi could no longer pay attention to his students or his family.

According to Rumi, Shams had a deep knowledge of alchemy, astronomy, theology, philosophy and logic. Rumi's son Sultan Walad in his writings tells us that Shams was "a man of learning and wisdom and eloquence and composition".

Relationship with Mawlana

Hazrat Shams and Maulana Rumi were inseparable and it is said that the two spent days, even months, together in a state of mystical communion. One biographer describes Mawlana's spiritual transformation at the hands of Hazrat Shams:

Hazrat Shams' relationship with Mawlana was unique in a sense it wasn't the traditional master-disciple kind of relationship. Mawlana was already an accomplished scholar and teacher in his own right, with a following of his own. Hazrat Shams talks about his apparent unwillingness or dilemma to behave in the manner of a shaykh in his writings:

"You know I have never acted shaykh-like, unmindful of your station, and said "I'm going here whether you like it or not and if you are mine, you'll come with me." No, I do not demand whatever is difficult for you." (Maqalat 761)

I need it to be apparent how our life together is going to be. Is it brotherhood and friendship or shaykh-hood and discipleship? I don't like this. Teacher to pupil? (Maqalat 686)

I first came to Mawlana with the understanding that I would not be his shaykh. God has not yet brought into being on this earth one who could be Mawlana's shaykh; he would not be a mortal. But nor am I one to be a disciple. It's no longer in me. Now I come for friendship, relief. It must be such that I do not need to dissimulate (nefaq). Most of the prophets have dissimulated. Dissimulation is expressing something contrary to what is in your heart. (Maqalat 777)

Despite his reluctance to act in the manner of shaykh, Mawlana Jalaluddin Rumi reserved great respect for him, as a student would show a teacher:

In my presence, as he listens to me, he considers himself - I am ashamed to even say it - like a two-year-old child or like a new convert to Islam who knows nothing about it. Amazing submissiveness! (Maqalat 730)

At times Mawlana would read the works of others for guidance and inspiration. However, Hazrat Shams told Mawlana that tasawwuf (Sufism) must be practised rather than merely being studied - "You want to discover through learning; but it requires going and doing" (Maqalat 128).

Therefore, he saw extensive knowledge as perhaps an impediment on the spiritual path:

"This multi-talented scholar, well-versed in fiqh and the principles and details of the law! These have no relationship to the path of God and the path of the Prophets. Rather, they cloak him from it. (Maqalat 361)"

He thus initiated a spiritual transformation in Mawlana Rumi. He reports Mawlana as saying: "Since I have become acquainted with you these books have become lifeless in my eyes." (Maqalat 186)

Shams:

I knew that no one understood me, not even my father.

Sham's father once said:

"You are not a madman fit to be put in a madhouse, nor are you a monk to be put in a monastery. I just don't know what you are!"

Shams replied:

"You know, father, I can tell you what it is like. Once a duck egg was put under a hen to be hatched. When the egg hatched, the duckling walked along with the mother hen until they came to a pond. The duckling took a nice dip in the water. But the hen stayed on the bank and clucked.

Now, my dear father, after having tried the sea I find it my home. If you choose to stay on the shore, is it my fault? I am not to be blamed."

The Wine

One day Molavi invited Shams Tabriz to his home. Shams accepted the invitation, but after he arrived there asked for a glass of wine. Jalaluddin Rumi astonished: "Do you drink wine?" "Yes" Shams answered.

- "but I didn't know!"

- "You know now, so bring some wine."

- "But it is too late, how can I bring it?"

- "Ask one of your servants."

– "But how can I ask them to wine? You know it is not appropriate for me."

– "So, go and buy some wine yourself."

– "People know me in this city, how can I go to wine-sellers' neighborhood?"

– "If I am your guest, you should bring some wine for me, because I cannot eat nor drink without wine."

That was how Jalaluddin Rumi took a bottle and went to wine-sellers' neighborhood. Nobody noticed him until he entered the neighborhood. "What is Molavi here for?" people asked themselves and followed him. They saw that he bought a bottle of wine from the only open store and came out from the bar.

So, a number of people followed him and asked the others to join them. After a while a large number of people gathered; therefore, one of his adversaries shouted: "O people, Sheikh Jalaluddin Rumi your liturgist just bought a bottle of wine."

People began to curse and insult Molavi. At this time, Shams arrived and shouted: "why are you insulting your liturgist? The bottle is vinegar not wine; O people!"

When they discovered the truth, they kissed Molavi's hands again."

"Why did you played with me tonight?" Jalaluddin Rumi asked. "I arranged it, because you should have known that what you have is just a mirage. You thought that having respect between common people is an eternal wealth. Now you experienced that a bottle of wine will ruin all of it in just a minute. If your wealth was what you lost in a minute tonight, so rely on something else."

With Love

One day Rumi was reading next to a large stack of books.Shams Tabrizi passing by, asked him, "What are you doing?"

Rumi scoffingly replied, "Something you cannot understand."

On hearing this, Shams threw the stack of books into a nearby pool of water. Rumi hastily rescued the books and to his surprise they were all dry.

Rumi then asked Shams, "Why did you do this?" To which

Shams replied:
"Mevlana, this is what you cannot understand"
"You will learn by reading but you will understand with love."

Shams Tabrizi Quotes

"Love is a travel. All travellers whether they want or not are changed. No one can travel into love and remain the same."

— Shams Of Tabriz

"Love is like a question, it expects answers."

— Shams Of Tabriz

"Nothing kills the soul that commands to evil like seeing the beauty of the hearth."

— Shams Of Tabriz

"A life without love is of no account. Love has no labels, no definitions. It is what it is. Love is the water of life."

— Shams Of Tabriz

"We are each an unfinished work of art both waiting and striving to be completed."

— Shams Of Tabriz

"The path to the Truth is a labour of the heart, not of the head. Make your heart your primary guide! Not your mind. Meet, challenge and ultimately prevail over your nafs with your heart. Knowing your ego will lead you to the knowledge of God."

— Shams Of Tabriz

"If you are insulted, if you are accused, if they gossip about you, don't say anything bad. Don't be the one who sees the shame, be the one who corrects it."

— Shams Of Tabriz

"We can only learn and advance with contradictions. The faithful inside should meet the doubtful. The doubtful should meet the faithful. Human slowly advances and becomes mature when he accepts his contradictions."

— Shams Of Tabriz

"If the human being is a proud and honorable creature, he shouldn't forget to act that way, even if he falls, even if the whole world is against him, even if he ends as a slave."

— Shams Of Tabriz

"Do not worry about tricks and cheaters. If some people are trying to trap and hurt you, God is also trapping them. Hole diggers will always fall in their holes. No bad remains unpunished, and no good remains without being awarded, so have faith in justice and let the rest be."

— Shams Of Tabriz

"If you expect respect from others, show it first to yourself. You can't expect from others what you don't give to yourself."

— Shams Of Tabriz

"To get closer to Truth and Right, we need a beautiful and soft heart."

— Shams Of Tabriz

"Be sure that someday you'll praise and thank God for your unanswered prayers that once you had wept for them."

— Shams Of Tabriz

"Intellect takes you to the door, but it doesn't take you into the house."

— Shams Of Tabriz

"A life without love is a waste. Should I look for spiritual love, or material, or physical love?, don't ask yourself this question. Discrimination leads to discrimination. Love doesn't need any name, category or definition. Love is a world itself. Either you are in, at the center... either you are out, yearning."

— Shams Of Tabriz

"It is never late to ask yourself "Am I ready to change my life, am I ready to change myself?".

— Shams Of Tabriz

"However old we are, whatever we went through, it is always possible to reborn. If each day is a copy of the last one, what a pity! Every breath is a change to reaborn. But to reborn into a new life, you have to die before dying."

— Shams Of Tabriz

"If words come out of the heart, they will enter the heart, but if they come from the tongue, they will not pass beyond the ears."

— Shams Of Tabriz

"Whatever happens in your life, no matter how troubling things might seem, do not enter the neighbourhood of despair. Even when all doors remained closed, God will open up a new path only for you. Be thankful! It is easy to be thankful when all is well. A sufi is thankful not only for what he has been given but also for all that he has been denied."

— Shams Of Tabriz

"The chemistry of mind is different from the chemistry of love. The mind is careful, suspicious, he advances little by little. He advises " Be careful, protect yoursel" Whereas love says "Let yourself, go!" The mind is strong, never falls down, while love hurts itself , falls into ruins. But isn't it in ruins that we mostly find the treasures? A broken heart hides so many treasures."

— Shams Of Tabriz

"How we see God is a direct reflection of how we see ourselves. If God brings to mind mostly fear and blame, it means there is too much fear and blame welled inside us. If we see God as full of love and compassion, so are we".

— Shams Of Tabriz

"Instead of resisting to changes, surrender. Let life be with you, not against you. If you think 'My life will be upside down' don't worry. How do you know down is not better than upside?"

— Shams Of Tabriz

"A life without love is of no account. Don't ask yourself what kind of love you should seek, spiritual or material, divine or mundane, eastern or western...divisions only lead to more divisions. Love has no labels, no definitions. It is what it is, pure and simple. Love is the water of life. And a lover is a soul of fire! The universe turns differently when fire loves water."

— Shams Of Tabriz

"The universe is a complete unique entity. Everything and everyone is bound together with some invisible strings. Do not break anyone's heart; do not look down on weaker than you. One's sorrow at the other side of the world can make the entire world suffer; one's happiness can make the entire world smile."

— Shams Of Tabriz

"Don't search for heaven and hell in the future. Both are now present. Whenever we manage to love without expectations, calculations, negotiations, we are indeed in heaven. Whenever we fight, hate, we are in hell."

— Shams Of Tabriz

"This world is like a mountain.
Your echo depends on you.
If you scream good things,
the world will give it back.
If you scream bad things,
the world will give it back.
Even if someone says badly about you,
speak well about him.
Change your heart to change the world."

— Shams Of Tabriz

"A good man complains of no one; he does not look to faults."

— Shams Of Tabriz

"Most of conflicts and tensions are due to language. Don't pay so much attention to the words. In love's country, language doesn't have its place. Love's mute."

— Shams Of Tabriz

"Don't judge the way other people connect to God; to each his own way and his own prayer.

— Shams Of Tabriz

God does not take us at our word. He looks deep into our hearts. It is not the ceremonies or rituals that make a difference, but whether our hearts are sufficiently pure or not."

— Shams Of Tabriz

"The summary of the advice of all prophets is this;Find yourself a mirror."

— Shams Of Tabriz

"It is pointless trying to know where the way leads. Think only about your first step, the rest will come."

— Shams Of Tabriz

"Every breath is a chance to reborn spiritually. But to be reborn into a new life, you have to die before dying."

— Shams Of Tabriz

"Surrendering is not a weakness. At the contrary it is strength. The surrender stops living in boiling water and starts living in a secure place."

— Shams Of Tabriz

"The real dirt is not outside,
but inside, in our hearts.
We can wash all stains with water.
The only one we can't remove is the grudge and the bad intentions sticking to
our hearts."

— Shams Of Tabriz

"Woe on the one whose eyes do not sleep but whose heart does sleep!"

— Shams Of Tabriz

"You have to live with the people in hypocrisy for them to stay happy with
you."

— Shams Of Tabriz

"Instead of resisting to changes, surrender. "

— Shams Of Tabriz

"Let life be with you, not against you."

— Shams Of Tabriz

"If you think 'My life will be upside down' don't worry. How do you know down is not better than upside?"

— Shams Of Tabriz

"A good man complains of no one; he does not look to faults."

— Shams Of Tabriz

"A life without love is of no account."

— Shams Of Tabriz

"Don't ask yourself what kind of love you should seek, spiritual or material, divine or mundane, eastern or western…divisions only lead to more divisions."

— Shams Of Tabriz

"Love has no labels, no definitions.
It is what it is, pure and simple.
Love is the water of life.
And a lover is a soul of a!
The universe turns differently when fire loves water. "

— Shams Of Tabriz

"The universe is a complete unique entity. Everything and everyone is bound together with some invisible strings.

Do not break anyone's heart; do not look down on weaker than you. One's sorrow at the other side of the world can make the entire world suffer; one's happiness can make the entire world smile. Most of conflicts and tensions are due to language. Don't pay so much attention to the words. In love's country, language doesn't have its place. Love's mute"

— Shams Of Tabriz

"Wherever you go, east, west, north or south, think of it as a journey into yourself! The one who travels into itself travels the world."

— Shams Of Tabriz

"When everyone is trying to be something, be nothing. Range with emptiness. Human should be like a pot. As the pot is hold by its emptiness inside, human is hold by the awareness of his nothingness."

— Shams Of Tabriz

"The whole universe is sum up in the Human Being. Devil is not a monster waiting to trap us, He is a voice inside. Look for Your Devil in Yourself, not in the Others.Don't forgeT that the one who knows his Devil, knows his God."

— Shams Of Tabriz

"It is pointless trying to know where the way leads. Think only of the first step. The rest will come."

— Shams Of Tabriz

"No matter what people call you, you are just who you are. Keep to this truth. You must ask yourself how is it you want to live your life. We live and we die, this is the truth that we can only face alone. No one can help us. So consider carefully, what prevents you from living the way you want to live your life?"

— Shams Of Tabriz

"We believe that God sees us from above But He actually sees us from the inside".

— Shams Of Tabriz

"You will learn by reading, but you will understand with love."

— Shams Of Tabriz

"You can be everything in life but the important thing is to be a good person."

— Shams Of Tabriz

"Intellect takes you to the door, but it doesn't take you into the house."

— Shams Of Tabriz

"There are more fake guides, teachers in the world than stars. The real guide is the one who makes you see your inner beauty, not the one who want to be admired and followed."

— Shams Of Tabriz

"Patience is not sitting and waiting, it is foreseeing. It is looking at the thorn and seeing rose, looking at the night and seeing the day. Lovers are patient and know that the moon needs time to become full."

— Shams Of Tabriz

"You can study God through everything and everyone in the universe, because God is not confined in a mosque, synagogue or church. But if you are still in need of knowing where exactly His abode is, There is only one place to look for Him: in the heart of a true lover."

— Shams Of Tabriz

"Most of problems of the world stem from linguistic mistakes and simple misunderstanding. Don't ever take words at face value."

— Shams Of Tabriz

When you step into the zone of love, language, as we know it becomes absolute. That which can not be put into words can only be grasped through silence."

— Shams Of Tabriz

"Loneliness and solitude are two different things. When you are lonely, it is easy to delude yourself into believing that you are on the right path. Solitude is better for us, as it means being alone without feeling lonely. But eventually it is the best to find a person who will be your your mirror. Remember only in another person's heart can you truly see yourself and the presence of God within you."

— Shams Of Tabriz

"Patience does not mean to passively endure. It means to look at the end of process. What does patience mean? It means to look at the thorn and see the rose, to look at the night and see the dawn. Impatience means to be shortsighted as to not be able to see the outcome."

— Shams Of Tabriz

"East, west, south, or north makes little difference. No matter what your destination, just be sure to make every journey a journey within. If you travel within, you'll travel the whole wide world and beyond."

— Shams Of Tabriz

"The midwife knows that when there is no pain, the way for the baby cannot be opened and the mother cannot give birth. Likewise, for a new self to be born, hardship is necessary. Just as clay needs to go through intense heat to become strong, Love can only be perfected in pain."

— Shams Of Tabriz

"The quest for love changes user. There is no seeker among those who search for love who has not matured on the way. The moment you start looking for love, you start to change within and without."

— Shams Of Tabriz

"There are more fake gurus and false teachers in this world than the number of stars in the visible universe. Don't confuse power-driven, self-centered people with true mentors. A genuine spiritual master will not direct your attention to himself or herself and will not expect absolute obedience or utter admiration from you, but instead will help you to appreciate and admire your inner self. True mentors are as transparent as glass. They let the light of God pass through them."

— Shams Of Tabriz

"Try not to resist the changes, which come your way. Instead let life live through you. And do not worry that your life is turning upside down. How do you know that the side you are used to is better than the one to come?"

— Shams Of Tabriz

"God is busy with the completion of your work, both outwardly. He is fully occupied with you. Every human being is a work in progress that is slowly but inexorably moving toward perfection. We are each an unfinished work of art both waiting and striving to be completed. God deals with each of us separately because humanity is fine art of skilled penmanship where every single dot is equally important for the entire picture."

— Shams Of Tabriz

"It's easy to love a perfect God, unblemished and infallible that He is. What is far more difficult is to love fellow human being with all their imperfections and defects. Remember, one can only know what one is capable of loving. There is no wisdom without love. Unless we learn to love God's creation, we can neither truly love nor truly know God."

— Shams Of Tabriz

"Real faith is the one inside. The rest simply washes off. There is only one type of dirt that cannot be cleansed with pure water, and that is the stain of hatred and bigotry contaminating the soul. You can purify your body through abstinence and fasting, but only love will purify your heart."

— Shams Of Tabriz

"The whole universe is contained within a single human being-you. Everything that you see around, including the things that you might not be fond of and even the people you despise or abhor, is present within you in varying degrees. Therefore, do not look for Sheitan outside yourself either. The devil is not an extraordinary force that attacks from without. It is an ordinary voice within. If you set to know yourself fully, facing with honesty and hardness."

— Shams Of Tabriz

"If you want to change the ways others treat you, you should first change the way you treat yourself, fully and sincerely, there is no way you can be loved. Once you achieve that stage, however, be thankful for every thorn that others might throw at you. It is a sign that you will soon be showered in roses."

— Shams Of Tabriz

"Fret not where the road will take you. Instead concentrate on the first step. That is the hardest part and that is what you are responsible for. Once you take that step let everything do what it naturally does and the rest will follow. Don't go with the flow. Be the flow."

— Shams Of Tabriz

"We were all created in His image, and yet we were each created different and unique. No two people are alike. No hearts beat to the same rhythm. If God had wanted everyone to be the same, He would have made it so. Therefore, disrespecting differences and imposing your thoughts on others is an amount to disrespecting God's holy scheme."

— Shams Of Tabriz

"When a true lover of God goes into a tavern, the tavern becomes his chamber of prayer, but when a wine bibber goes into the same chamber, it becomes his tavern."

— Shams Of Tabriz

"In everything we do, it is our hearts that make the difference, not our outer appearance."

— Shams Of Tabriz

"Sufis do not judge other people on how they look or who they are. When a Sufi stares at someone, he keeps both eyes closed instead opens a third eye (the eye that sees the inner realm)."

— Shams Of Tabriz

"Life is a temporary loan and this world is nothing but a sketchy imitation of Reality. Only children would mistake a toy for the real thing. And yet human beings either become infatuated with the toy or disrespectfully break it and throw it aside. In this life stay away from all kinds of extremities, for they will destroy your inner balance. Sufis do not go to extremes. A Sufi always remains mild and moderate."

— Shams Of Tabriz

"The human being has a unique place among God's creation. "I breathed into him of My Spirit," God says. Each and every one of us without exception is designed to be God's delegate on earth. Ask yourself, just how often do you behave like a delegate, if you ever do so? Remember, it fells upon each of us to discover the divine spirit inside and live by it."

— Shams Of Tabriz

"Hell is in the here and now. So is heaven. Quit worrying about hell or dreaming about heaven, as they are both present inside this very moment. Every time we fall in love, we ascend to heaven. Every time we hate, envy or fight someone we tumble straight into the fires of hell."

— Shams Of Tabriz

"Each and every reader comprehends the Holy Qur'an on a different level of tandem with the depth of his understanding. There are four levels of insight. The first level is the outer meaning and it is the one that the majority of the people are content with. Next is the Batin – the inner level. Third, there is the inner of the inner. And the fourth level is so deep it cannot be put into words and is therefore bound to remain indescribable."

— Shams Of Tabriz

"The universe is one being. Everything and everyone is interconnected through an invisible web of stories. Whether we are aware of it or not, we are all in a silent conversation. Do no harm. Practice compassion. And do not gossip behind anyone's back – not even a seemingly innocent remark! The words that come out of our mouths do not vanish but are perpetually stored in infinite space and they will come back to us in due time. One man's pain will hurt us all. One man's joy will make everyone smile."

— Shams Of Tabriz

"Whatever you speak, good or evil, will somehow come back to you. Therefore, if there is someone who harbours ill thoughts about you, saying similarly bad things about him will only make matters worse. You will be locked in a vicious circle of malevolent energy. Instead for forty days and nights say and think nice things about that person. Everything will be different at the end of 40 days, because you will be different inside."

— Shams Of Tabriz

"The past is an interpretation. The future is on illusion. The world does not more through time as if it were a straight line, proceeding from the past to the future. Instead time moves through and within us, in endless spirals. Eternity does not mean infinite time, but simply timelessness. If you want to experience eternal illumination, put the past and the future out of your mind and remain within the present moment."

— Shams Of Tabriz

"Destiny doesn't mean that your life has been strictly predetermined. Therefore, to live everything to the fate and to not actively contribute to the music of the universe is a sign of sheer ignorance. The music of the universe is all pervading and it is composed on 40 different levels. Your destiny is the level where you play your tune. You might not change your instrument but how well to play is entirely in your hands."

— Shams Of Tabriz

"The true Sufi is such that even when he is unjustly accused, attacked and condemned from all sides, he patiently endures, uttering not a sing bad word about any of his critics. A Sufi never apportions blame. How can there be opponents or rivals or even "others" when there is no "self" in the first place? How can there be anyone to blame when there is only One?"

— Shams Of Tabriz

"If you want to strengthen your faith, you will need to soften inside. For your faith to be rock solid, your heart needs to be as soft as a feather. Through an illness, accident, loss or fright, one way or another, we are all faced with incidents that teach us how to become less selfish and judgmental and more compassionate and generous. Yet some of us learn the lesson and manage to become milder, while some others end up becoming even harsher than before…"

— Shams Of Tabriz

"Nothing should stand between you and God. No imams, priests, rabbits or any other custodians of moral or religious leadership. Not spiritual masters and not even your faith. Believe in your values and your rules, but never lord them over others. If you keep breaking other people's hearts, whatever religious duty you perform is no good. Stay away from all sorts of idolatry, for they will blur your vision. Let God and only God be your guide. Learn the Truth, my friend, but be careful not to make a fetish out of your truths."

— Shams Of Tabriz

"While everyone in this world strives to get somewhere and become someone, only to leave it all behind after death, you aim for the supreme stage of nothingness. Live this life as light and empty as the number zero. We are no different from a pot. It is not the decorations outside but the emptiness inside that holds us straight. Just like that, it is not what we aspire to achieve but the consciousness of nothingness that keeps us going."

— Shams Of Tabriz

"Submission does not mean being weak or passive. It leads to neither fatalism nor capitulation. Just the opposite. True power resides in submission a power that comes within. Those who submit to the divine essence of life will live in unperturbed tranquillity and peace even the whole wide world goes through turbulence after turbulence."

— Shams Of Tabriz

"In this world, it is not similarities or regularities that take us a step forward, but blunt opposites. And all the opposites in the universe are present within each and every one of us. Therefore the believer needs to meet the unbeliever residing within. And the nonbeliever should get to know the silent faithful in him. Until the day one reaches the stage of Insane-I Kamil, the perfect human being, faith is a gradual process and one that necessitates its seeming opposite: disbelief."

— Shams Of Tabriz

"This world is erected upon the principle of reciprocity. Neither a drop of kindness nor a speck of evil will remain unreciprocated. For not the plots, deceptions, or tricks of other people. If somebody is setting a trap, remember, so is God. He is the biggest plotter. Not even a leaf stirs outside God's knowledge. Simply and fully believe in that. Whatever God does, He does it beautifully."

— Shams Of Tabriz

"God is a meticulous dock maker. So precise is His order that everything on earth happens in its own time. Neither a minute late nor a minute early. And for everyone without exception, the clock works accurately. For each there is a time to love and a time to die."

— Shams Of Tabriz

"It is never too late to ask yourself, "Am I ready to change the life I am living? Am I ready to change within?" Even if a single day in your life is the same as the day before, it surely is a pity. At every moment and with each new breath, one should be renewed and renewed again. There is only one-way to be born into a new life: to die before death."

— Shams Of Tabriz

"While the part change, the whole always remains the same. For every thief who departs this world, a new one is born. And every descent person who passes away is replaced by a new one. In this way not only does nothing remain the same but also nothing ever really changes. For every Sufi who dies, another is born somewhere."

— Shams Of Tabriz

"A life without love is of no account. Don't ask yourself what kind of love you should seek, spiritual or material, divine or mundane, Eastern or Western. Divisions only lead to more divisions. Love has no labels, no definitions. It is what it is, pure and simple. Love is the water of life. And a lover is a soul of fire! The universe turns differently when fire loves water."

— Shams Of Tabriz

"You learn by reading but understand by LOVE".

— Shams Of Tabriz

"Shams, my body is a candle touched with fire."
— Rumi

Printed in Great Britain
by Amazon